Blessed Chiara Badano

Her Secrets to Happiness

Blessed Chiara Badano

Her Secrets to Happiness

GERALDINE GUADAGNO, Author

LORETTA RAUSCHUBER, Illustrator

NCP

New City Press

Hyde Park, New York

Published in the United States by New City Press
202 Comforter Blvd., Hyde Park, NY 12538
www.newcitypress.com

© 2021 New City Press

Blessed Chiara Badano
Her Secrets to Happiness

Cover and design by Loretta Rauschuber

Library of Congress Control Number: 2021943842

ISBN: 978-1-56548-702-4 paper
ISBN: 978-1-56548-703-1 e-book

We thank the Chiara Badano Foundation
for its help in bringing this book to fruition.

To V.R.A., M.G., and T.C.B. with love.
I want to live the secrets well, for you.

Geraldine Guadagno

Everything I've ever done has been inspired by my parents, Helen and Ray Rauschuber. Thank you for being a model of what eternal love truly looks like.

I'd also like to thank my spiritual mother, Chiara Lubich, who has been a source of light for my path.

In my early twenties, I "left everything" to follow God as a consecrated member of the Focolare Movement. Due to some circumstances at that moment, this also meant leaving behind my students who were preparing for the sacrament of Confirmation at St. Mary's, my hometown parish. I loved them very much! Then, over the years I understood that when it comes to giving everything, or really, anything, to God, he never forgets. Through my illustrations, God has opened a door for me to once again give my small but meaningful contribution to all those preparing for the sacrament of Confirmation. This book is for you!

Loretta Rauschuber

"Perhaps it is our similar age or our shared Italian heritage or the battles with cancer my own family members have faced, but I've felt a certain closeness to Blessed Chiara ever since first hearing her story. What a delight to learn more about her through this book! I knew she was an excellent role model for young people, but this book reveals the depths of her faith and intellect. Adults and young people alike will benefit from discovering how Chiara learned the secrets to happiness at such a young age."

Amy J. Cattapan, DM, Ed.D.

"The story of Chiara Luce Badano is the story of the next generation of saints. Young and old alike will be inspired by the story of a saintly teenager who gave her life to others and offered up her suffering. In a saddened and depressed world, we need Chiara's secrets to happiness. She shines as a bright light in the midst of darkness."

Fr. Edward Looney, author of
A Lenten Journey with Mother Mary

"What a perfect little introduction to Bl. Chiara Badano! This short but thorough biography is so readable I flew through it in a day, and it comes nicely illustrated, for a bonus. A book for anyone of any age who wants to know more about this inspiring Italian teen."

Corinna Turner, author of *The Boy Who Knew (Carlo Acutis)* and the Carnegie Medal-nominated *I Am Margaret* series

"In her new book *Blessed Chiara Badano: Her Secrets to Happiness*, Geraldine Guadagno captures the spirit of Blessed Chiara's simple yet profound spirituality for a new generation to know and follow. Illustrated by Loretta Rauschuber, this book compellingly shares Chiara's light and love for a new generation of believers."

Lisa M. Hendey, author of *I'm a Saint in the Making*

"Every child will see a bit of themselves in Chiara and realize the rewards of living life with an eye on Jesus. Through the joys and the sorrows, the accomplishments and the difficulties, Blessed Chiara models goodness and virtue by living the Gospel. Her advice to stay focused on the present moment should comfort and guide us on the path to happiness."

Doreen McAvoy, author of *Secrets in September*, and Catholic high school librarian and teacher of 9th Grade theology

Contents

In Her Own Words

L et's stop for a moment to reflect on the meaning of our lives. . . . Often, human beings do not live their life because they are immersed in a time that does not exist, either in the memory or regrets of the past or projected into the future. In reality, the only time that anyone possesses is the present moment, which should be lived completely taking full advantage of it. By living in this way, people will feel free because they are no longer crushed by the anguish of the past and worries about the future.

Certainly, it is not easy to reach this goal and it requires constant effort to remain in this reality. . . . The only way to make the most of time is to make sense of our every action, large or small. A person could give meaning to everything by going beyond selfishness and giving value to everything by doing it for others. Perhaps we would have to give a new intention to each of our actions and we would certainly feel more fulfilled and become more aware of the value of life as a precious gift that cannot and should not be wasted nor burned up in sterile selfishness and useless ambition.[1]

Chiara Badano

---

1. Chiara Badano Foundation, *In My Staying Is Your Going*, trans. Bill Hartnett and Maria Blanc (Hyde Park, NY: New City Press, 2021).

Introduction

"Be happy, because I am," said the young woman on her sickbed. Chiara Badano, almost nineteen years old, had discovered the secrets of happiness. Those secrets had nothing to do with being well, much less being rich, beautiful, or famous, doing whatever she wanted or having whatever she wanted. She held these secrets in her heart and put them into practice every day. These secrets, which had been shared with her and which she shared with others, helped her live an extraordinary life and create a legacy of light and love that continues to this day. However, her story begins much earlier, with her parents, Ruggero and Maria Teresa, and a lot of prayer.

Chapter One

Chiara's Apple and the Table: A Transgression and a Glimpse of Light

Truck driver Ruggero Badano and his wife Maria Teresa lived in Sassello, a hilly northern Italian village known for its traditional cookies and porcini mushrooms. For eleven years, Ruggero and Maria Teresa had prayed to have a child, even praying at a shrine dedicated to Our Lady. At long last, on October 29, 1971, they had a baby girl and named her Chiara (kee-AR-ah).

Ruggero and Maria Teresa said, "She was our child, but even more than that, she was a child of God."

Maria Teresa left a job in a factory to stay home and raise their daughter, who grew up happy and healthy. There was something special about Chiara, too. At times, she seemed to have a deep, insightful understanding of things. Her gift of understanding may have helped her to grasp the secrets.

Of course, like all children, Chiara sometimes misbehaved, needed to be taught right from wrong, and struggled to do the right thing. Once she brought home an apple from a neighbor's orchard. She had taken it without the neighbor's permission. Her mother explained why Chiara had to give it back immediately and apologize. Embarrassed, Chiara hesitated at first, but with her mother's guidance and encouragement, she returned the neighbor's apple. Ruggero also disciplined Chiara, but always with love and reason.

The Gospels made an impression on Chiara at an early age. Maria Teresa would read bedtime stories (fairy tales and the like) to Chiara. However, she would often read the Gospels to Chiara too, and she taught Chiara to pray. Chiara showed how much she understood one day when her mother asked her to clear the table.

"I don't want to," Chiara said. She folded her arms and walked away. But then she turned back, saying: "How does that

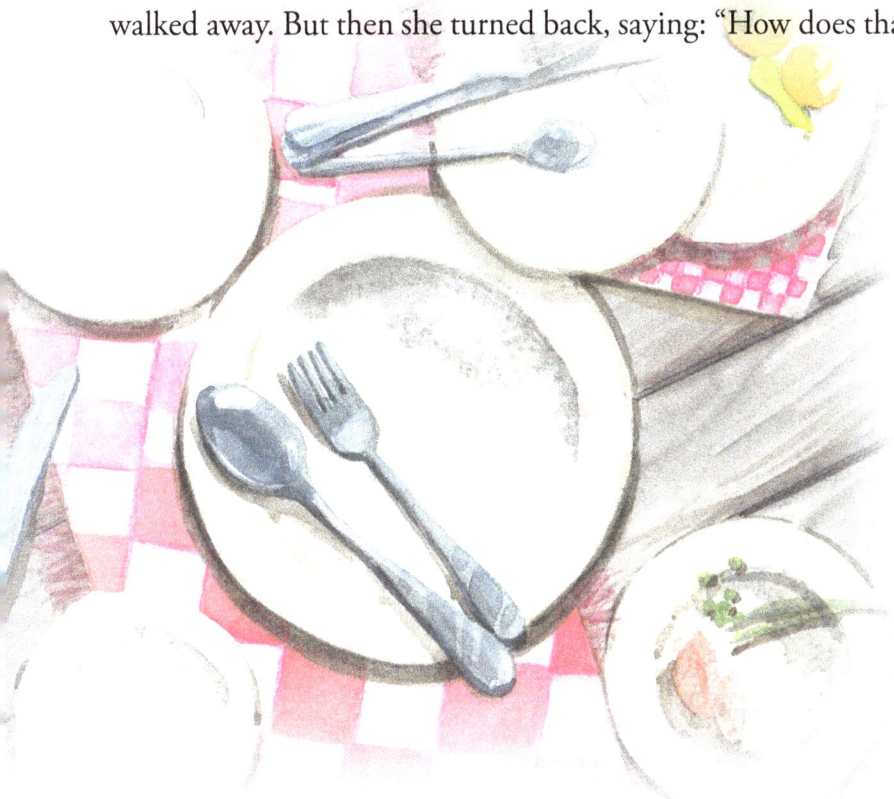

story from the Gospel go, about the father who asks his son to go to the vineyard?"[2] Remembering the parable about the two sons and which one did his father's will—meaning God's will—she cleared the table (see Matthew 21:28–31).

2. Kelly, Christine, "Ordinary, Extraordinary Life," *Living City*, March 2010, 6–7.

oing the will of God was one of the secrets to happiness that she would embrace, and it was hidden in the Gospel. Chiara and her parents would have to see the Gospel in a new light in order to discover this secret and others.

This light began dawning when Chiara's parents heard about the Focolare (foh-coh-LA-ray) Movement. It was a group of people, of all ages and walks of life, who wanted to love God. They tried to put Jesus' words into action every day. Maria

Teresa and Ruggero decided to attend the Focolare "Family Fest" in Rome in 1979, and brought eight-year-old Chiara with them. They arrived late to the crowded sports arena where the meeting was being held.

After they had found their seats, Chiara said, "Papa, I'm hungry." Ruggero didn't know what to do. They hadn't brought any food with them. Then, suddenly, someone nearby handed him a sandwich. Someone else offered them an orange drink. These "strangers" made the Badano family happy. Most of all, they loved the Badanos in the way that Jesus would have loved them. Maria Teresa and Ruggero were won over. After returning home, Chiara and her parents all tried to love one another as Jesus would in order to live in unity with Jesus among them (see Matt 18:20). However, their love could not remain confined only to their own family.

In 1980, Chiara attended one of the Focolare's children's meetings, and was won over, too. She wrote a letter to the founder of the Focolare, Chiara Lubich. "I have rediscovered the Gospel in a new light. . . . I want to make this magnificent book the only aim in my life,"[3] she said. This was the first of many letters that she would write to the woman who shared her name.

---

3.   Kelly, "Ordinary, Extraordinary Life," 6.

Chapter Two

The Least, also Known as Jesus

Whether or not parents are wealthy—and the Badanos, who lived on a truck driver's salary, were certainly not wealthy—an only child tends to accumulate things, including toys. Chiara certainly did, even though her parents did their best not to spoil her.

hen Chiara was four years old, her mother said, "You have so many toys—why don't you give some away to poor children who have none?"

"No," Chiara said. "They're mine." Then a few minutes later, she said, "Mama, can I have a plastic bag?"

As Chiara slid her best toys into the bag, her mother said, "But those are the new ones."

She replied, "Mama, you can't give old broken toys to poor children." Again, Chiara showed a lot of understanding, even at the tender age of four. She made a start at living Jesus' words in Matthew 25:30–45, particularly, "Truly I tell you, just as you did it to one of the least of these, . . . you did it to me."

Jesus identified himself with the needy and the vulnerable, those whom society might consider worthless, useless, undesirable, and even detestable. No matter their circumstances, everyone always has value to God, who creates each person in his own image and likeness. Jesus, who is God, asked that "the least" be valued and loved, with a love that was expressed in actions. He promised to consider each action as if it were done to him. He also modeled how to love: Jesus, who had asked his disciples to love *as* he had loved (see John 13:34), laid down his life for each and every person from the beginning of time until the end of time. In order to love others as Jesus did, we may not have to die physically for them, but we may have to die to—that is, give up—our own ideas and plans or our concern for ourselves. As Pope Francis has said, we need to move from the "I" to the "we."

At age seven, while preparing to receive her First Holy Communion, Chiara mentioned wanting to offer acts of love to Jesus.

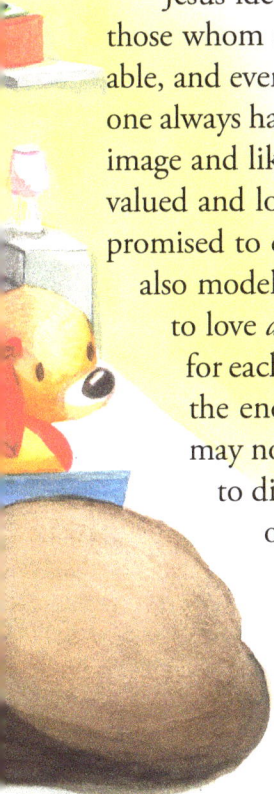

But even before this, in kindergarten, after seeing a documentary about poor and suffering children in Africa, she told her teacher and her classmates, "From now on, we will take care of them."[4] Chiara never forgot these children. Later, as a teenager, she often saved her allowance in order to send the children money. She also dreamed of becoming a pediatrician so that she could go to Africa and give them medical help.

4. Chiara Badano Foundation,
    In My Staying Is Your Going.

When Chiara was twelve, one of her classmates had scarlet fever, and all the students were afraid to visit her. That is, all except Chiara. She wrote in her diary: "With my parents' permission I am going to take her the homework, so that she doesn't feel lonely."[5]

Chiara visited the elderly in nursing homes too. One day, a resident seemed sad. Chiara talked with her and discovered that the woman thought that her laundry was missing and might have been stolen. In reality, she was mistaken. All of her laundry was accounted for. However, under the circumstances, Chiara thought that the best way to love this woman as Jesus would love her was by offering to take her laundry home to do it.

After a friend's mother and grandmother became ill, Chiara treated them like family and invited them for meals. She asked her mother to use their best tablecloth, "because Jesus is coming to visit us today."[6]

There came a time when Chiara's own grandfather, who lived nearby, needed someone to watch over him at night. As Maria Teresa and Ruggero took turns doing so, they became exhausted. Chiara offered to stay with her grandfather instead. She kept asking until her parents finally agreed. Though she stayed awake the entire night, Chiara didn't seem tired at all during school the next day.

When she was in her late teens, Chiara was asked by the local Focolare leaders if she would take charge of some younger girls living in the area. They were new to the spirituality of unity, but wanted to put it into practice. Chiara agreed and put her heart into the task. She kept in close contact with the girls, writing to them, calling them, and sending them little gifts.

5.   Michele Zanzucchi, *Chiara Luce: A Life Lived to the Full* (London: New City), 21.

6.   Zanzucchi, *Chiara Luce*, 25.

All of this may seem like a lot of work and responsibility, but Chiara also had friends and plenty of fun throughout her life. She loved music, singing, and dancing. She was athletic and enjoyed tennis, skating, and swimming. Her hometown of Sassello was less than an hour from the coast by car, and Chiara often swam in the Ligurian Sea. Still, she would face challenges.

Chapter Three
Human Nature and the World

Two things are inescapable during our lives: our human nature and—unless we are retreating to a cloister or monastery—the influence of the world.

Most of Chiara's time was not spent playing and laughing with the other Focolare children, called "Gen."[7] Among other things, she had to attend school. Chiara's good behaviors—attending Mass and faith formation classes and helping anyone in need—earned her some teasing. Some students called her "the little nun." The day before a field trip, her classmates even excluded her by pairing up to sit together and leaving her without a seatmate for the bus. This made Chiara feel sad at first, but then she remembered Jesus' suffering out of love for us, and she accepted her situation happily. The next morning, Chiara received what she called "the hundredfold" (see Matthew 19:29) when a girl asked to sit with her. The girl's friend, it seemed, had chosen to sit with someone else during the trip. This incident helped Chiara make a decision "to love those who are annoying to me."[8]

---

7. "Gen" is short for "New Generation," a term that the Focolare uses to signify that even children are made "new" by putting the words of the Gospel into practice. See 2 Corinthians 5:17: "If anyone is in Christ, there is a new creation: everything old has passed away; see, everything has become new!" Similar terms are used to describe families and other groups in the Focolare.

8. Florence Gillet, *15 Days of Prayer with Blessed Chiara Badano* (Hyde Park, NY: New City Press), 61.

Good behavior can be challenging. In her mid-teens, Chiara had trouble keeping herself from swearing. She also said, "The TV often tempts me with films that are not really nice. Each time, I ask Jesus for special help." She would also think of her Gen friends in those moments, because she knew that they were trying to overcome similar tendencies and temptations.[9]

In 1985, when Chiara was fourteen, the Badano family moved to Savona to be closer to Ruggero's job and to Chiara's high school. The change wasn't easy. She wrote in her diary:

> These have been difficult days for me, because after the move to Savona several problems have arisen, including school and feeling homesick for Sassello which I was very fond of.(...) It was difficult to say yes to [Jesus], but I tried, starting by giving a hand to my mother (...) [and] studying my lesson because it is God's will . . . My life was transformed. And then the news about the Gen meetings seemed like special help from Jesus to always be up.[10]

For Chiara, always being "up" meant always loving the people around her.

---

10. Chiara Badano Foundation, *In My Staying Is Your Going.*

Chiara worked hard in school. As subjects became more difficult, she spent more time studying and seldom saw her friends. Chiara also had a personality clash with a teacher at one point.

Then one year, despite her best efforts, she failed her exams. It was a serious setback. In July 1986, she wrote to a friend: "As you will have heard, I failed and it was really big suffering for me. (…) I took a long time to get back up and, still now, when I think about it, I start to cry a little."[11] Despite knowing a secret that Focolare founder Lubich had revealed even to the youngest Gen, Chiara struggled with this failure. We'll learn more about this secret in the next chapter.

---

11. Chiara Badano Foundation, *In My Staying Is Your Going.*

Chiara sometimes disagreed with her parents. One argument involved her curfew on weekends, when they usually visited Sassello.

Chiara enjoyed staying out late at a café with friends. Maria Teresa and Ruggero, being protective, at first imposed a curfew that left her seething. While her friends talked and ate ice cream at the café, she had to sit at home.

She complained, "I feel like Cinderella who, at midnight, had to run off. . . . Don't you trust me?"[12] Yes, her parents trusted her, but they weren't so sure about some others in the group. Then, realizing how much this bothered Chiara, they suggested a compromise: If there was an important discussion going on, she could decide to stay. But the next time, she needed to return home by 10 p.m. After thinking it over, Chiara agreed.

---

12. Zanzuchhi, *Chiara Luce*, 28.

hiara never needed to be the center of her friends' attention. She didn't discuss Gen activities or Jesus with them, either.

When Maria Teresa expressed surprise that Chiara said nothing to her friends about God, Chiara replied, "I don't have to talk about God, I have to give God . . . first and foremost by placing myself in a position of listening, by the way I dress, but above all by the way I love them."[13] Since God is Love, Chiara "gave" God to her friends by loving them, by making their concerns her own.

As for young men, quite a few were interested in Chiara. She even began falling in love with someone. However, the relationship only lasted a few weeks. Chiara's best friend, Chicca (kee-kah) Coriasco said that Chiara ended it with him "in a very mature, very direct way."[14]

Later, Chiara told her mother, "I realized that perhaps for him, things were different: maybe he just wanted to hang around with me."[15] When we have feelings of romantic love for someone and that person doesn't feel the same way about us, it hurts. It may even break our heart. Although Chiara didn't say so directly, this situation may have caused her a lot of pain.

In addition to changing schools as a teenager, Chiara also moved to another Gen group. This change was difficult for her, too. She didn't know some of the other teens, and she had a different group leader. At one point, Chiara skipped two of their meetings in a row. She said little about it. She faced an unspoken question: Would she, or would she not, keep choosing to live her secrets? Would she keep on doing God's will and loving

13. Chiara Badano Foundation, *In My Staying Is Your Going*.

14. Zanzucchi, *Chiara Luce*, 33.

15. Zanzucchi, *Chiara Luce*, 33.

others as Jesus asked in the Gospel? It would be much easier to live only for herself, thinking of her own desires, and following the latest trends and fashions.[16]

Chiara said, "I was nearly 'lost.'. . . Our Ideal [God] was becoming secondary."[17] But things would change, suddenly and dramatically.

---

16. People in the Focolare Movement, also known as the Work of Mary, take the Blessed Virgin Mary as their model in Christian life, in the way that they maintain and decorate their homes and especially in the way that they dress—with simplicity, neatness, cleanliness, and modesty so that others will feel comfortable around them. They sometimes refer to imitating Mary and her virtues as "going against the current" of popular culture. Most of all, through loving God and their neighbor, they aim to bring Jesus into the world again, just as Mary once brought him into the world.

17. Zanzucchi, *Chiara Luce*, 29.

Chapter Four
The Secret of the Abandoned One

*a*fter Chiara's very first meeting with the Gen in September 1980, when she was nine years old, she wrote to Chiara Lubich: "We have started our adventure: to do the will of God in the present moment. With the Gospel in our hands, we will do great things."[18] A friend of Chiara's from those early days remembered her as high-spirited, always smiling and having "a pure look in her eyes."[19]

Whenever the Gen met, they also learned about Jesus. They learned about his prayer at the Last Supper. In that prayer, he asked the Father to make all of his disciples one. Jesus wanted them to be united in his love, loving him and loving one another. Together with the Gen, Chiara learned the secret of this unity.

The secret to being united was to love Jesus Forsaken (in Italian, *Gesù Abbandonato*). As he hung upon the cross, for a moment Jesus felt that God, his Father, had left him alone. Despite knowing that the Father had not left him and that the Father never leaves us either, Jesus knew the human feeling of abandonment by God because of sin. He felt the human loss of God's presence and of Paradise (see Genesis chapter 3). Then he cried, "My God, my God, why have you forsaken me?" (Matthew 27:46). That was the moment when Jesus suffered the most. It was also the moment when Jesus loved us the most. The Focolare's founder, Chiara Lubich, understood some special things about that moment.

---

18. Zanzuchhi, *Chiara Luce*, 20.

19. Zanzucchi, *Chiara Luce*, 20.

First, because God exists in the eternal Now, or the "eternal present moment," to him everything is happening now, including the moment of Jesus' feeling abandoned out of love for us. This means that Jesus can be loved in his moment of forsakenness, right now, by us.

Lubich also understood that Jesus united us with himself and reunited us with the Father through his suffering and death on the cross. Moreover, he experienced every type of human suffering, even though he is God. Though this was a great mystery, it helped her to accept suffering in order to love people as Jesus did. She would go beyond her own pain—a headache, for example, or being misunderstood—to love the other person. Or, she shared their pain in order to love them. For instance, if someone was sad, she would be sad with them. Lubich called this "loving Jesus Forsaken." Often, when she loved him, and was united with the suffering person, their suffering would turn into joy. But Lubich made sure to love Jesus Forsaken for himself alone, not for that joy. She chose him as her one Spouse on earth. She explained her understanding when she met with the Gen, or through letters, which the Gen leaders would read to them.

*a*fter a Gen 3 Congress—a meeting of Gen ages nine to fifteen from all over the world—Chiara Badano, at only eleven years old, wrote:

> I rediscovered Jesus Forsaken in a special way. I experienced him in every person who passed by me. This year I have made a new resolution to see Jesus Forsaken as my spouse and to welcome him joyfully and, above all, with all the love possible.[20]

Less than five months later, she wrote: "I have understood that I can find [Jesus Forsaken] in those who are far from God . . . and that I have to love him in a very special way, without any self-interest."[21] Chiara had chosen to live the secret of loving Jesus Forsaken. She had no way of knowing then how he would come to her. No one had any idea what he would ask of this lively and intelligent girl.

After learning the secret of Jesus Forsaken, Chiara made a point of loving people when they suffered: her friend with scarlet fever, the woman in the nursing home, and many other people, young and old. She recognized her failed exams as Jesus Forsaken in disguise. Even so, for a while, she had a hard time going beyond the pain. Then, Jesus Forsaken turned up again, soon after that moment when she had felt that she was giving God the second place in her life.

During the summer of 1988, when Chiara was sixteen, she was in the middle of a tennis game when a sharp pain stabbed her shoulder. It hurt so badly that she dropped her racket.

20. Zanzucchi, *Chiara Luce*, 22.

21. Zanzucchi, *Chiara Luce*, 22.

Doctors thought she had a cracked rib. But the pain persisted and she ran a fever. Tests soon revealed that Chiara had a tumor from a rare bone cancer.

At that time, Chiara was only told that she was very ill. She took the news calmly. As the months went by, she endured more examinations, treatments, hospital stays, and times of being confined to bed at home, as well as times of remission. Rather than focus on herself, Chiara turned toward others. While in the hospital, she met another girl who was ill. Chiara befriended her and would often take long walks with her around the hospital.

When her parents asked her to rest, Chiara said, "I'll be able to sleep later on."[22]

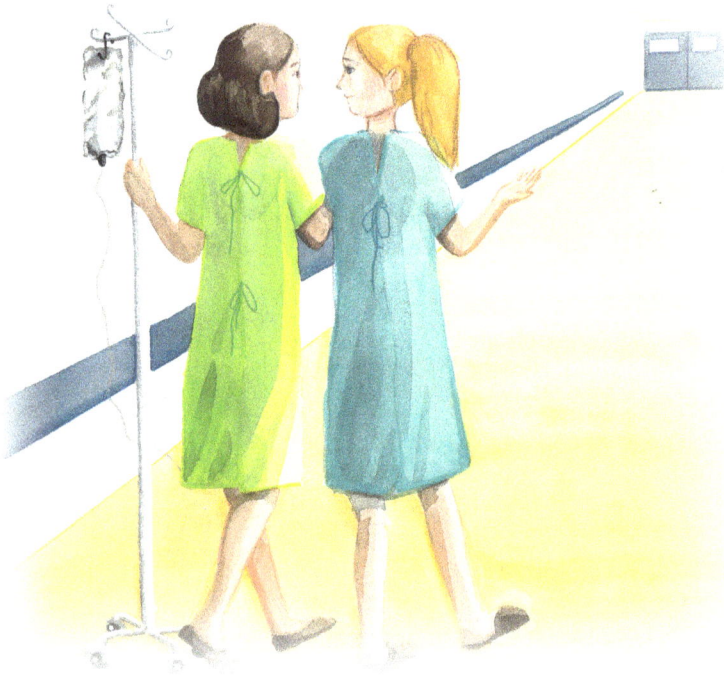

---

22. Zanzucchi, *Chiara Luce*, 35.

Chiara even looked at the illness as a sort of game that God was playing with her. She said:

> The important thing is doing God's will. Maybe I had plans for myself, but God thought of this. . . . You can't even imagine what my relationship with Jesus is now. . . . I feel that God is asking me something more, something greater. Maybe I could stay in this bed for years. . . . I don't know. I only care about doing God's Will, doing that well, in the present moment, keeping on playing God's game.[23]

As a Gen, Chiara had learned that God has a specific plan or design for each person's life. Although she had dreams and ambitions, she understood that what God wanted of her and for her might be very different from what she had in mind. God's will is most often revealed in the circumstances of our lives, especially those circumstances that we can't change.

She exchanged letters with her best friend, Chicca. Through reading and rereading those letters, Chicca understood that, despite the hardships, Chiara "wanted to be 100% authentic."[24]

Soon, Chiara needed an operation. She and her parents stayed at a friend's home in Turin, so that they could be near the hospital. Though she hoped that she would be cured, Chiara knew that things weren't going well.

23. Chiara Badano Foundation, *In My Staying Is Your Going.*

24. Zanzucchi, *Chiara Luce,* 35–36.

*a*s soon as she woke from the operation, she asked, "Why, Jesus?" Then, after a few minutes, she said, "If you want it, Jesus, then so do I."[25] Later, she asked the doctor about her prognosis. He explained how serious her illness was, and that she needed chemotherapy, which would make her hair fall out. This knowledge presented her with another crucial choice.

After arriving back at their friend's house, Chiara couldn't give her mother the news.

"Not now," she said. "Let's not talk about it now." Then she threw herself onto the bed and closed her eyes. Knowing that Chiara was struggling, Maria Teresa silently suffered with her. After twenty-five minutes, Chiara smiled and said, "Now we can talk." In her heart, she had said "yes" once again to Jesus Forsaken.

Chiara wrote to Lubich, "Jesus has sent me this illness just at the right moment. He sent it to me so that I could find him again."[26]

Later, as she lost her shiny hair, Chiara offered each lock, saying, "For you, Jesus." She would have more occasions to repeat this phrase.

---

25. Zanzucchi, *Chiara Luce*, 37.

26. Zanzucchi, *Chiara Luce*, 37.

Chapter Five
Patient Endurance and Joy

"May you be made strong with all the strength that comes from his glorious power, and may you be prepared to endure everything with patience, while joyfully giving thanks to the Father, who has enabled you to share in the inheritance of the saints in the light" (Colossians 1:11–12).

Soon, Chiara had another surgery, more painful than the first. Shortly after returning home from the hospital, she became weak and lethargic. When Maria Teresa called the doctor and described the symptoms, he told her to get Chiara back to the hospital immediately. But it was almost Christmas, and Chiara wanted to spend the holiday at home with her family, no matter the consequences.

Only after her mother whispered, "This is the will of God," did she agree to go and receive the blood transfusion that she so desperately needed.

The next day was Christmas Eve. Maria Teresa stayed at Chiara's side, and they did their best to love each other as Jesus would. Cardinal Saldarini of Turin visited the ward that afternoon and stopped in to see Chiara.

Struck by her appearance, he remarked, "You have a marvelous light in your eyes. How come?"

After a moment's hesitation, Chiara replied, "I try to love Jesus."[27]

Meanwhile, the youth of the Focolare stayed so close to Chiara and her parents that her father felt surrounded by a

---

27. Zanzucchi, *Chiara Luce*, 38.

large family. Like Chiara, Maria Teresa, and Ruggero, the young people knew that the most important thing was to love Jesus Forsaken so that they could be united and have his presence among them. They recognized that Chiara, in her suffering, was living Jesus' experience of abandonment on the cross. They kept in close contact with her and she with them.

Though the young people usually thought that they were visiting to cheer Chiara up, they always found that she lifted them up.

Her friend Ferdinando said, "And yet Chiara didn't come out with any extraordinary words, nor did she write pages and pages. . . . She just loved."[28] Despite her illness, Chiara did her best to love all of her friends the way that Jesus would love them. However, Chiara needed her friends, too. In a letter to them, she wrote: "I feel your unity very strongly, your offerings, your prayers which allow me to renew my 'yes,' moment by moment."[29]

Chiara kept a list of her personal possessions, which she saw not as exclusively her own, but also as belonging to her friends. If they had a need, she was always ready to give anything she had. In this way, they could all live as the first Christians did, where "there was not a needy person among them" (Acts 4:34).

28. Zanzucchi, *Chiara Luce*, 39.

29. Zanzucchi, *Chiara* Luce, 39.

To strengthen their spiritual bond, Chiara also shared with her friends a mystical experience. In a tape recording that she made for them, she spoke of seeing "a beautiful lady with a radiant smile"[30] while enduring a round of spinal injections. The lady appeared out of nowhere and grasped Chiara's hand. Then the woman vanished, but left Chiara feeling joyful and peaceful, with no trace of fear. Chiara had a strong desire to thank God for this lady's "visit." She wondered if it had been a coincidence, but went on to say:

> And above all with that light, which without exaggerating, I would say was supernatural. She was like an angel—an angel that Our Lady put next to me.

---

30. Zanzucchi, *Chiara Luce*, 41.

It was a very profound moment of God. . . . I understood something: if we were always ready, . . . how many signs God would send us. I also understood just how many times God passes near us and we don't realize it.[31]

Chiara had some other special visitors, too. One day, a large number of young men tried to sneak into her hospital room. They were members of the singing group Gen Rosso. Chiara had planned to attend one of their concerts, but since illness prevented her, they came to her instead. They sang three songs for Chiara, and one seemed to refer to her directly. Everyone was moved by it. Then, a member of the hospital staff carried in Chiara's dinner.

Gazing at the crowd in the room, the hospital worker said, "Of course, we don't have enough for everyone."[32]

Perhaps Chiara's most special visitor was Jesus in the Eucharist. One morning, after she had spent hours praying, "Come, Lord Jesus," a priest arrived to give her Holy Communion. She was elated.

The joy that Chiara radiated affected her doctors and nurses, raising their thoughts to God, although some of them were atheists. Even her parents felt that they were on a supernatural plane when they were with her. As they did their best to love one another and keep Jesus among them, they had joy, the joy that often comes with his presence, and so much joy that Chiara began singing some of the Gen songs one night. Ruggero was a bit concerned that she might disturb the other patients, but he didn't want to interrupt her.

31. Zanzucchi, *Chiara Luce*, 42.

32. Maria Beatrice Cerrino, personal interview, August 9, 2019.

Once, however, when Chiara was at home again, Ruggero wondered if she was putting on an act. After leaving her bedroom, he spied on Chiara through the keyhole. Much to his amazement, even though she was alone and in a lot of pain, she was still smiling.

The late and final stages of cancer are often extremely painful. To get any relief, patients frequently need regular doses of morphine, a powerful drug. A person isn't weak, cowardly, or undisciplined if they need it. God doesn't want anyone to suffer, especially when medical remedies are available. However,

Chiara made a choice, and God seemed to honor her choice by giving her a special gift, or grace.

Her legs became paralyzed, and their muscles often contracted, which hurt. It also hurt to sit up while speaking with visitors, but Chiara refused morphine.

She said, "It takes away my lucidity, and all I have to offer Jesus is suffering. . . . If I'm not lucid, what sense has my life got?"[33] In spite of her pain, visitors never guessed what sitting up cost her.

Chiara saw her sufferings as Jesus purifying her, preparing her for heaven.

She told her mother, "Jesus is using bleach to remove all my stains. The bleach burns. . . . Then when I go to heaven, I'll be as white as snow."[34]

Ruggero asked Chiara, "How do you manage to live like this?"

"Oh, Papa," she said. "You take a minute, divide it into four parts, and then you offer. . . . You offer with all your strength." As Chiara focused intensely, made offerings to Jesus Forsaken, and lived just fifteen seconds at a time, God enabled her to endure the pain without morphine.

If someday we are seriously ill, we should not expect God to give us the same sort of gift as he gave Chiara. Consider the saints. Jesus gave the stigmata to a few of them, but not others. Some saints are also martyrs, but many are not. God's design or plan for each life is as unique as we are. It brings to mind St. Paul's words in 1 Corinthians 12:8–11:

33. Zanzucchi, *Chiara Luce*, 43.

34. Gillet, *15 Days of Prayer with Blessed Chiara Luce Badano*, 99.

To one is given through the Spirit the utterance of wisdom, and to another the utterance of knowledge, . . . to another faith, . . . to another gifts of healing, . . . to another the working of miracles, to another prophecy, to another the discernment of spirits, to another various kinds of tongues, to another the interpretation of tongues. All these are activated by one and the same Spirit, who allots to each one individually just as the Spirit chooses.

Throughout this time, Chiara remained humble, writing: "Jesus has allowed this trial, but the merit is his if I manage to accept it. . . . I have very little to do with it."[35]

When she was confined to bed at home and cared for by her parents and her aunt Mimma, Chiara kept up with the Gen by telephone. When "Genfest," the international youth festival, was coming up, Chiara wrote to one of the women in charge of it. In her letter, Chiara offered "her nothingness" for the youth who would attend, so that the Holy Spirit would inspire and enlighten them. Chiara saw herself as nothing in comparison to God.[36]

She also exchanged more letters with Lubich, who gave her a Gospel verse to call her own: "Those who abide in me and I in them bear much fruit" (John 15:5). Christians speak of God "pruning" them—as a gardener would prune a tree's branches—so that they can bear more fruit, perhaps by loving others more. He takes away anything that the person no longer needs, which can be as painful to them as a cut. Chiara's last pruning would indeed produce abundant fruit.

---

35. Zanzucchi, *Chiara Luce*, 50.

36. Chiara Badano Foundation, *In My Staying Is Your Going*.

Chapter Six
Called by a New Name

In the previous chapter, we learned that God doesn't want anyone to suffer. Why then, do so many people suffer, as Chiara did? If God is Love, if he is all-good and all-powerful, then why does he allow evil, suffering, and death?

The answer is a bit complicated, because suffering is a great mystery.

Through the sin of our first parents, pain and death entered the world (see Genesis chapter 3). But God also promised to send a Redeemer: his only Son, Jesus. Through Jesus' obedience to God the Father in his Passion, death, and Resurrection, our sins were forgiven. We were delivered from death and given the gift of eternal life (see Romans 5:12–18). Jesus has already won the final victory over Satan, who is his adversary and ours. At the end of time, when Jesus comes in glory, we will enjoy that victory at last.

Notice, however, that God the Father did not spare Jesus from the suffering of the cross or from death. What was the greatest evil ever done? The killing of God's own Son. What was the end result of that evil act? Our greatest good: our redemption!

When God *allows* certain things to happen, he always has a greater good in mind. Because he loves us, he gives us freedom, free will with which to choose his will or to reject it.[37]

---

37. See Libreria Editrice Vaticana, *Catechism of the Catholic Church*, (Liguori, MO: Liguori Publications, 1994), paragraphs 309–314.

What is God's will? To love him and our neighbor always. If we reject God's will, we will probably sin. Then we will have to endure the consequences, which most likely will include some pain and suffering. (But if we repent, turn toward God, and ask for forgiveness,[38] heaven rejoices.)

Again, though, there are many who are innocent, like Chiara, who do their best to do God's will, and yet suffer. Jesus too was innocent. By uniting their pain with that of Jesus on the cross, these people can participate in his redemption of the world. Nothing was lacking in Jesus' perfect sacrifice on the cross, but we can add our sufferings to his for the salvation of the world. Our offering may be tiny in comparison, but God will accept it.

Once we have made our offering, it's healthy and reasonable to use medicine for relief. For example, if we have a headache, we can offer up a moment of pain right away by saying, "For you, Jesus Forsaken." Next, we can take a headache medicine, and then go on to look for ways to love our neighbor.

We may never see the results, the "greater good," of our offering in this life. That doesn't mean that it has been useless, that nothing has happened or that something has been lost. God, who is never outdone in generosity, is in charge of the end results and will reward us in the next life. Again, Chiara provides us an example.

Chiara took each day as it came, accepting her suffering as permitted by God's will, but always hoping to be cured. When doctors could do no more to help, her only concern was remaining faithful to Jesus Forsaken. She wrote to Lubich, "I

---

38. Repentance is best expressed by receiving God's limitless mercy and forgiveness in the Sacrament of Reconciliation as soon as we can.

feel so small and the road ahead is so hard. Often I feel over-whelmed by suffering. . . . Yes, I will repeat with you, 'If you want it, Jesus, I want it too.'"[39] She included a photograph with this letter.

Lubich replied, "Your luminous face shows your love for Jesus. Chiara, don't be afraid to say your 'yes' to him, moment by moment. He will give you strength. . . . I too am praying for this and am always there with you." Because she felt transformed by the Gospel, Chiara had asked the Focolare founder for a new name. Lubich chose the word "Luce" (LOO-chay)—"light," in English—as her young friend's name.

She wrote: "It is the light of the Ideal which conquers the world. I send it with all my love."[40] The founder's love also helped Chiara Luce to continue loving. Like a pebble dropped into a pond, that love would ripple out toward many other people, perhaps more than Chiara Luce ever imagined.

39. Zanzucchi, *Chiara Luce*, 49.
40. Zanzucchi, *Chiara Luce*, 50.

Chapter Seven
Her Legacy Begins

Knowing that she would not recover, Chiara Luce made detailed plans and left nothing to chance. One of the first things that she did was order her parents to go out for Valentine's Day (in 1990).

She said: "Look into each other's eyes and say, 'I love you very much.' And don't come back before midnight." She said to her mother: "Remember that before I came along, there was Papa."[41]

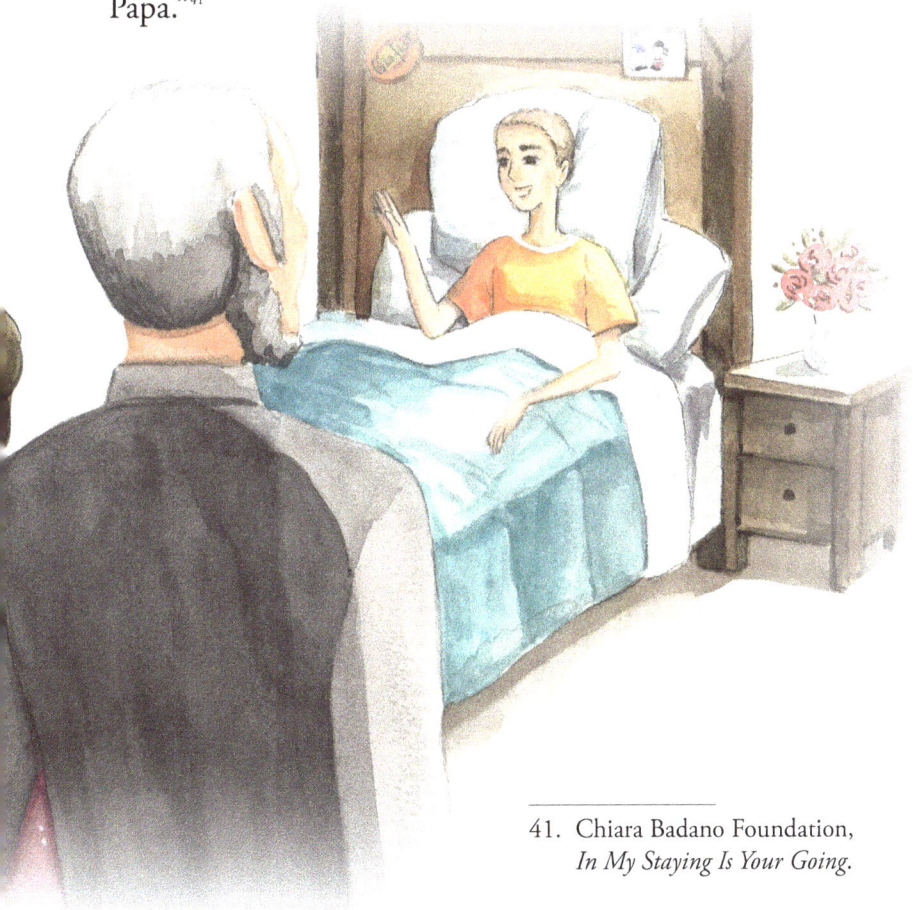

---

41. Chiara Badano Foundation, *In My Staying Is Your Going.*

Chiara Luce also asked her parents to donate her corneas to eye patients after her death. Her eyes were one of the few parts of her body unravaged by cancer and the treatments.

As for her funeral, Chiara Luce wanted to make it a celebration, a sort of wedding reception, because she had chosen Jesus Forsaken as her Spouse and would be united with him in heaven. She planned the music for the service together with her friend Chicca. She also wanted a simple white dress with a pink sash.

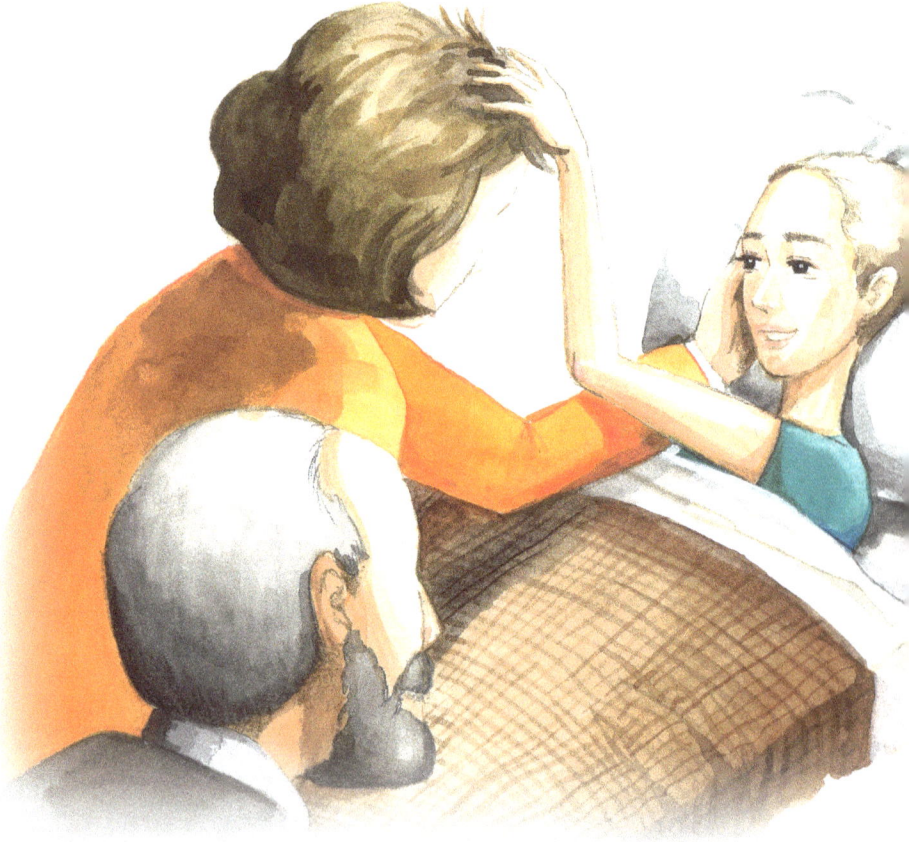

She told her mother, "And when you dress me, you must keep repeating, 'Now Chiara can see Jesus!'"[42]

There was one plan that Chiara Luce kept to herself, her own little secret, which was only discovered later: despite having given her entire savings to a friend going on a mission trip to Africa, she had somehow scraped together a bit more money. It was found in her bedroom, in a box marked "for the poor in Africa."

When the end finally came, she smiled at her parents.

Ruffling her mother's hair, she said, "Be happy, because I am." Then she closed her eyes and met Jesus. It was Sunday, October 7, 1990, about three weeks before what would have been her nineteenth birthday.

More than two thousand people attended Chiara Luce's funeral, which was as joyful as she had planned.

She had shared her secrets—doing the will of God in the present moment, loving others as Jesus loves us, and embracing Jesus Forsaken—and her journey with the Gen, right up to the last moment. Some Gen commented on her choice of God and the Gospel. One said, "For the first time, I was certain of the love of God."

Another said, "Many things unite us . . . but there is something else I would like to do together with Chiara Luce: become a saint."

Another addressed a prayer to her: "You, who like me had dreams, . . . help me to make my life into a masterpiece."[43]

God has seemed to answer some of those aspirations and prayers, including prayers for a dying boy, through Chiara Luce's intercession.

---

42. Chiara Badano Foundation, *In My Staying Is Your Going*.

43. Zanzucchi, *Chiara Luce*, 55–56.

Chapter Eight
Beatification and Beyond

Less than nine years after Chiara Luce's death, the bishop of Acqui Terme, Livio Maritano, who had known her personally, petitioned the Holy See to begin the beatification process. During that time, people of all ages had been making pilgrimages to Chiara Luce's final resting place, her family's chapel in the Sassello Cemetery. They had filled a basket there with notes and letters to her. The Focolare Movement Center in Rome had also received countless letters from people who changed their lives, rediscovered their faith, or were blessed with special graces after learning about Chiara Luce.

With the Holy See's approval, documents and testimonies from seventy-two witnesses to Chiara Luce's life were gathered, along with her own writings. Within a year, Bishop Maritano delivered twelve volumes of information to the Vatican.

On July 3, 2008, Pope Benedict XVI declared Chiara Luce "Venerable."

In January 2009, the Congregation for the Causes of Saints consulted several doctors about the healing of a young boy in Trieste, Italy. In 2001, the boy had contracted a strain of meningitis that was nearly always fatal. His doctors had expected him to die within forty-eight hours. The boy's uncle visited Chiara Luce's grave and begged for her intercession. He also asked everyone he knew to pray for her intercession. Afterward, his nephew suddenly improved and made a full recovery. The independent doctors convened by the Church came to a unanimous decision: the boy's remarkable recovery could not be explained by medical science. Cardinals and bishops who also reviewed the case agreed with their findings. The Holy Father did, too.

Before 2009 was over, Pope Benedict XVI signed the decree approving the miracle. Then Chiara Luce was declared "Blessed."

On September 25, 2010, the rite of beatification was celebrated in Rome at the Church of Our Lady of Divine Love (*Madonna del Divino Amore*). It was attended by 25,000 people, young and old, from more than seventy countries. A celebration followed that included music, theater, and the testimony of witnesses. It also reached across the globe, thanks to livestreaming. Even the media in some Muslim countries commented on Chiara Luce after the Mass of Thanksgiving for the Beatification, which was broadcast the next day.

In 2019, the Chiara Badano Foundation created an annual award program for artwork inspired by Chiara Luce's life, for the purpose of making her better known and presenting her as a model for today's youth. Young people and adults between the ages of ten to thirty-five can enter and submit any type of art, from paintings to dances to songs to cartoons.

Blessed Chiara Luce's life continues to touch many other lives around the world, all because she learned the mysterious secrets of happiness, love, and unity.

At the time of this writing, her feast day is October 29.

To become even better acquainted with Blessed Chiara Luce, visit chiarabadano.org.

THE END

Discussion Questions

1. What did Blessed Chiara Luce do in those moments when she failed to love others? After all, isn't this how we live the words of Jesus in the Gospel?

2. Why might Chiara Luce have had a brief period in which she seemed to give other things more importance than God?

3. Other holy women, such as Saint Catherine of Siena and Saint Thérèse of Lisieux, have spoken about Christ as the Spouse of their soul. Chiara Luce chose Jesus Forsaken as her Spouse. What do you think this means?

4. After she became ill, how did Chiara Luce spend her time? What might have happened if she had spent her time differently?

5. Chiara Luce said, "Maybe I had plans for myself, but God has thought of this." What do you think she meant?

6. How important was sharing a spirituality to Chiara Luce and her family? Without the support and community of other believers, would they have been as successful at living out their Christian faith? (Think about this 1982 commentary on the Gospel, written by Chiara Lubich: "If we live in isolation from one another, we cannot resist the pressures of the world for long, while in mutual love we find an environment capable of protecting an authentic Christian life."[44])

7. Chiara Luce's "secrets" were to live for others, to do the will of God, and to embrace Jesus Forsaken in order to love others and be united with them. How will you put these secrets into action in your own life?

---

44. Focolare Movement International, "You have already been cleansed by the word I have spoken to you," https://www.focolare.org/en/download/you-have-already-been-cleansed-by-the-word-i-have-spoken-to-you-jn-153/, accessed June 23, 2020.

Acknowledgements

Geraldine Guadagno

Throughout the years, I have been blessed by my family in countless ways. Their love, patience, encouragement, prayers, faith in God, and faith in me have been priceless. The same can be said about many close friends, some of whom are writers, who believe in my work and tell me in no uncertain terms to keep going. Then there are those acquaintances, some of them professionals, who, even as they lend me their expertise, now and again find a way to challenge me. Without them, how would I do my best work? Without my friend and collaborator, the talented and dedicated Loretta Rauschuber, as illustrator, this book would not have come to life. To each one of you, and all of you, although it hardly seems enough, thank you from the bottom of my heart. To my Lord and Savior, without whom I am nothing and can do nothing, thank you for Blessed Chiara Luce Badano and for sending me the words, again. I hope that I have done your will, and that this little book pleases you and brings you more glory, praise, and thanksgiving.

Loretta Rauschuber

I really want to thank Helen Roh—she was there for me every step of the way. She did so with love and patience and encouragement, mentoring me with her years of professional experience. You have these illustrations because of her.

Bibliography

Calo, Maria A. *Chiara Luce Badano: A Teen's Life and Beatification.* Hyde Park, NY: Luminosa Audiovisual Center, 2011. DVD.

Cerrino, Maria Beatrice. Personal Interview. August 9, 2019.

Chiara Badano Foundation. http://www.chiarabadano.org/life/?lang=en.

Chiara Badano Foundation. *In My Staying Is Your Going.* Translated by Bill Hartnett and Maria Blanc. Hyde Park, NY: New City Press, 2021.

Focolare Movement International. "You have already been cleansed by the word I have spoken to you. (Jn 15:3)," https://www.focolare.org/en/download/you-have-already-been-cleansed-by-the-word-i-have-spoken-to-you-jn-153/.

Fondazione Chiara Badano. *Nel mio stare il vostro andare: Vita e pensieri di Chiara "Luce" Badano.* Rome: Città Nuova, 2019.

Gillet, Florence. *15 Days of Prayer with Blessed Chiara Luce Badano.* Hyde Park, NY: New City Press, 2015.

Kelly, Christine. "Ordinary, Extraordinary Life." *Living City,* March 2010.

Libreria Editrice Vaticana. "Providence and the scandal of evil." In the *Catechism of the Catholic Church,* paragraphs 309–314. Liguori, MO: Liguori Publications, 1994.

Swaim, Colleen. *Ablaze: Stories of Daring Teen Saints.* Liguori, MO: Liguori, 2011.

Zanzucchi, Michele. *Chiara Luce: A Life Lived to the Full.* London: New City, 2007.

New City Press

New City Press is one of more than 20 publishing houses sponsored by the Focolare, a movement founded by Chiara Lubich to help bring about the realization of Jesus' prayer: "That all may be one" (John 17:21). In view of that goal, New City Press publishes books and resources that enrich the lives of people and help all to strive toward the unity of the entire human family. We are a member of the Association of Catholic Publishers.

www.newcitypress.com
202 Comforter Blvd.
Hyde Park, New York

Periodicals
Living City Magazine
www.livingcitymagazine.com

Scan to join our mailing list
for discounts and promotions
or go to www.newcitypress.com
and click on "join our email list."